WICF

Written and illustrated by
Mal Peet

Collins Educational

An imprint of HarperCollinsPublishers

Contents

Wicked

Darren McSweeney is wicked.
Show him a scab and he'll pick it.
Show him a stone and he'll chuck it.
Show him a worm and he'll tuck it
down the back of a girl from Year Three.

Darren McSweeney is wicked.
Got the new Beano? He'll nick it.
Lend him your felt-tip, he'll suck it.
He chewed all my gum and he stuck it
in the hair of the girl from Year Three.

Mind you –
she didn't half give him a kick in the knee.

Seagulls

They're easy to draw – a flat W
of white chalk
against the blue.

They slide easily
down slopes in the air
that we can't see.

There's very little they won't eat.
They'll swallow whole starfish
big as their feet.

They scream in rubbish dumps,
fighting for the smelliest,
tastiest lumps.

Their beaks are yellow knives.
There's something snaky
about their cold, yellow eyes.

Hard as I try,
I just can't like them;
I don't know why.

The Price

My Uncle Alan swears at the ref.
He swears at the linesmen, too.
He calls them totally blind and deaf
and curses them till his face goes blue.
It's embarrassing. I only stick it
because Uncle Alan buys my ticket.

The Loser

There was an old lady from Ottery
Who won two million pounds on the lottery;
She went down the town
To a pub called The Crown
And came home all giggly and tottery.

That same old lady from Ottery
Spent all she'd won on the lottery
On pearls for her cats,
Some very wild hats,
Silk knickers and perfume and pottery.

12

You Need Scissors, You Do

Miseryguts, Miseryguts,
why don't you smile?
There's a dark cloud behind you
big as a mile.

Miseryguts, Miseryguts,
you like feeling bad.
The worst time's the best time
you've ever had.

Miseryguts, Miseryguts,
give me no ifs, give me no buts,
there's a dark cloud behind you
as big as the moon;
it's tied to your wrist
like a fairground balloon.

Honest

The dentist said "This won't hurt. Just relax.
You won't feel this drilling at all.
It's really quite nice being flat on your back
with a needle stuck into your jaw.
And Mum's not the Tooth Fairy
and Dad's not Santa Claus."

Here's what I heard on the Six O'Clock News:
"The whole world is happy and peaceful today;
no-one is angry, no-one's confused.
Everyone's agreed not to fight any wars.
And Mum's not the Tooth Fairy
and Dad's not Santa Claus."

The Prime Minister got to his feet and he said:
"No-one is hungry, no-one is sick,
everyone's got a nice house and a bed.
No-one will ever be poor any more.
And Mum's not the Tooth Fairy
and Dad's not Santa Claus."

Eating raw carrots is good for your eyes.
Cheats never prosper. Cats have nine lives.
Your nose will grow long if you keep telling lies.
It's true, I know it, I know it because
Mum's *not* the Tooth Fairy
and Dad's *not* Santa Claus.

Couch Potato

My Aunt Nelly
watches telly
with her hands on her belly
and her feet on a stool.

One day the Council knocked down her flat,
just like that,
knocked it flat as a mat
for a new swimming pool.

When the dust cleared,
they found her still there,
watching the telly
with her hands on her belly
and her feet on a stool.

They took her away in the back of a truck
(she was still alive, by a stroke of luck)
to an Old Folks' Home called Sunnyside Farm
where she wouldn't come to any harm.

She's still there, is Auntie Nelly,
watching the telly
with her hands on her belly
and her feet on a stool.

Her favourite show is 'This is Your Life'.

Dave's Fleas

My friend David keeps pet fleas
who hide in small groups
at the back of his knees;
they're quick and they're canny
and anxious to please.
Dave's fleas can...

... skip and fight
ride a bike
drive a car
bop in a bucket
and jog in a jar
hold a sword
use a pen
do a dance
and count to ten
walk a tightrope
carry small fish
run a race
around a dish
suck your blood
and spit it out
stand on a pin-head
and not wobble about.
Just when you think they've had enough
they'll lift small weights
to show they're tough.

Dave *likes* his fleas. He likes them lots.
He doesn't care about his spots.

Watch it, because...

when I say I can sulk,
I don't mean
just go in a corner and skulk
with my bottom lip stuck out.
Oh no.
When I work a good sulk up,
a really strong one,
I can aim it like a gun,
blow the video,
put out the sun,
give you toothache,
start a headache,
flatten a rainbow,
cause an earthquake.
Once I sulked for seven hours
and drained the colour from a vase of flowers.
I could sulk a hole in space.
I'll sulk the nose right off your face.

I could sulk for England, I could.

After the Snow

After the snow
the white cat
from next door
crossed the lawn,
slow, slow.
Only her lemon eyes showed.

The black bird
on the white lawn
never saw
the cat from next door.
When he looked, I think
she must have blinked
and disappeared.

Now on the snow
you can read the story –
the small print
of the bird's claws
and the death sentence
of the white cat's paws.

Still on the snow,
just two black feathers,
a tiny drop of red,
and what's left
of the crust of bread
I'd thrown.

Just Do It

I believe in ghosts.
I like the idea
of long-ago people made of thin air
who walk through thick walls
like they're not even there.

I believe in fairy tales.
There's a world somewhere
of gingerbread houses, cartoon princesses,
hero princes who see off the rascals,
and happiness, sunsets, weddings and castles.

And, of course, I do believe
in the adverts they show on TV.
I can be a film star, too,
if I use the right shampoo.
You can be free just by buying a car.
What you wear matters, not who you are.
Want it. Eat it. Buy it. Buy *two*.
Get it. Just do it. Believe it, it's true.

Sinking Poem

The Owl and the Pussycat went to sea
in a poem by Edward Lear.
After a while
Owl said with a smile,
"This poem is leaking, I fear.

"Oh Pussy, dear Pussy, I really must fly,
there's water got into this verse;
besides, I've a hunch
I was meant for your lunch
or breakfast, or dinner, or worse."

The Vampire

The bathroom is locked. Inside is Count Dracula,
Lord of the Not Really Dead,
like a bat in his cloak, horrid, spectacular
with eyes like red fires in his head.

His claws and his fangs are pointed and cruel.
His victim will shudder with fear.
He can see in the mirror if he stands on a stool;
his reflection is perfect – it's simply not there.

His victim screams as he slides in the door,
her hands flying up to her throat;
"Billy, you monster! I've told you before –
don't use my make-up! And take off my coat!"